2006

blooming
twig books

www.bloomingtwigbooks.com

Other Books by Cynthia Blomquist Gustavson

Poetry

Sick-A-War Tree

The Battle Within

I Don't Write Love Poems

Scents of Place

Ruach

Poetry Therapy

In-Versing Your Life: A Poetry Workbook
For Self-Discovery and Healing

Fe-vers: Feeling Verses for Children

Fe-vers: Feeling Verses for Teens

Re-Versing the Numbers: A Poetry Workbook
For Eating Disorders

Con-Versing With God: Poetry For
Pastoral Counseling and Spiritual Direction

Spirituality

Human Spirit, Holy Spirit

Kingdom Words

www.cynthiagustavson.com
www.bloomingtwigbooks.com

RE-VERSING YOUR PAIN

A *Poetry Workbook for Those Living With Chronic Pain*

Poetry and Text by
Cynthia Blomquist Gustavson, MSW, LCSW, ACSW

blooming
twig books

NEW YORK

Several poems in this manuscript have previously appeared in <u>Scents of Place: Seasons of the St. Croix Valley</u>, by Cynthia Blomquist Gustavson. Published by Country Messenger Press, Marine on St. Croix, MN, copyright ©1987.

Several poems in this manuscript have previously appeared in <u>Where the Wind Comes From</u>, by Cynthia Blomquist Gustavson. Published by Holden Press, Tulsa, OK, copyright ©2001.

Several poems in this manuscript appear in <u>In-Versing Your Life</u>, <u>Ruach,</u> <u>The Battle Within</u>, <u>I Don't Write Love Poems</u>, and <u>Sick-a-War Tree</u>, by Cynthia Blomquist Gustavson. Published by Blooming Twig Books, East Setauket, NY, copyright ©2006.

The introduction to this manuscript first appeared in <u>Families in Society: The Journal of Contemporary Human Services</u>, May/June 2000, Vol. 81, No. 3.

Re-Versing Your Pain copyright ©2006 Cynthia Gustavson. Tulsa, Oklahoma.
www.cynthiagustavson.com
Published 2006 by Blooming Twig Books
3A Detmer Road
East Setauket, NY 11733
www.bloomingtwigbooks.com
1-866-389-1482
Catalog #: BT001

9 8 7 6 5 4 3 2
First Blooming Twig Books Edition 2006.

ISBN 0-9777736-7-1

DEDICATED TO BRITTA

CONTENTS

II. PRESENT

INTRODUCTION

USING POETRY AS THERAPY
Cynthia Blomquist Gustavson

Reprinted with permission from Families in Society:
The Journal of Contemporary Human Services,
May/June 2000, Vol. 81, No. 3.

It was 1987. My first book of poetry had just been published and I was a social worker/counselor at a clinic in Minnesota. Clients showed up in my office clutching folded scraps of paper upon which they had written their secret poetry. Timidly they unwrapped them, handed them to me, and said, "Does this mean anything?" To which I would reply, "You tell me what it means."

It was as though a dark closet had been opened. Clients who had been writing poetry secretly for years now openly admitted to its use. It was like Vice President Dole admitting he needed Viagra. Poetry. For romantic women and children and English teachers? Not any more. Poetry came of age as a survival tactic.

In that same year I attended a funeral of a close family friend. He was one of those people who deserved so much more than he ever got. A real saint. Everyone knew it, and it was hard to let go. When the minister asked if anyone present would like to share a thought with the group, two men came forward. Neither man knew the other, but each had written a poem he wanted to share at the funeral. Each prefaced his poem by saying he had not written poetry since primary school, and he didn't like doing it then, but in his grief he found his profound feelings could not be expressed in any other way except through poetry. And so each had picked up the pen and written a poem, and then felt the need to share it with others.

As I listened to the two men, and thought about their shared experience, I realized the inherent power of poetry. I knew I had been using it for self-discovery throughout my own life, my clients were sharing with me their own writings and now the stories of these two men solidified in my mind the therapeutic value of poetry. This was the beginning of my understanding of what we call "process poetry;" finding value and meaning in a poem, not just from the end product, but from the process of reading, thinking, feeling, debating, holding, and writing it.

I soon found others had also discovered this treasure. In 1980 the first National Association of Poetry Therapy conference had been held. And in 1987, the year I was finding my way into this discipline, the first issue of the Journal of Poetry Therapy was published.

Everyone has heard of art therapy and music therapy, but often when I mention poetry therapy, the listener thinks of it in the same ilk as aroma therapy or magnets. Let me attempt to rescue it from that categorization with an example.

A few years ago I was asked to do a poetry presentation at an alternative school in Shreveport, Louisiana. I was brought into a room in which 10 girls, between the ages of 13 and 16, were seated around a large table. I was informed that they were in this class because they had all given birth. I read them poetry for a while, and got them excited about poets such as Lillian Clifton and Maya Angelou. During the presentation I noticed one young girl appeared to be sleeping, her head on the table and her eyes closed. I asked the girls to do a classic poetry therapy exercise (devised by Kenneth Koch) with me. They were to write, "I used to be ... but now I am...," filling in the blanks with a metaphor from nature that would describe themselves.

I did not notice that the young girl with her head on the table was actually writing something on her paper. When it came time for her to share her writing I was prepared to skip her, but the teacher mentioned she had seen her writing. She asked her very nicely to read it. The girl was too shy, but asked the teacher to read her poem. It said, "I used to be a beautiful flower, but now I am a stem, because I am broken."

There was silence in the room. Every girl there understood the beauty and the truth of what she had written. When they started praising her and calling her a poet, she raised her head and started talking. She had been back from the birth of her baby for two weeks and this was the first time she had spoken to anyone. At the end of class I approached her and said how much I loved her poem. I also asked her to keep writing about her feelings, and eventually to write a poem using the formula, "I am. . . but I will be . . ."

I use this technique in therapy sessions often with people who are in transition. A young woman who was newly divorced wrote, "I used to be a whole garden of flowers, but now I am choked by weeds." A teenager suffering from depression wrote, "I used to be a free flowing river, but now I am the dam." This technique can also be used at the termination of therapy to summarize positive change. One client wrote, "I used to be an acorn, closed tight and hidden, but now I am an oak tree growing taller every day, giving shade and shelter to others."

This type of therapy can also be used developmentally, rather than clinically, by anyone who is seeking self-discovery and healing. In my book, *In-Versing Your Life: A Poetry Workbook for Self-Discovery and Healing,* (Families International, Inc. Milwaukee, WI. 1995; reprinted 2006, Blooming Twig Books) I paired 50 poems and exercises which enabled the reader to use these techniques for his/her own growth and understanding.

The most common type of poetry therapy used in both individual and group sessions is the introduction of a poem, or part of a poem, written by someone else, followed by a discussion of it. The best kind of poem for this use is one which has a universal understanding, has vivid images, is easy to understand, and is open-ended (not preachy.) Poems by Robert Frost, Mary Oliver, Emily Dickinson, and Carl Sandburg are a good place to begin to find appropriate poems. The poem must be matched to the client in areas such as emotional tone, cultural identity, gender issues, and developmental level.

Mary Oliver's poem "Wild Geese" starts with these lines:

> You do not have to be good.
> You do not have to walk on your knees
> for a hundred miles through the desert, repenting.
> (from New and Selected Poems. 1992. Beacon Press: Boston. p.110)

You can easily see that this poem might be used in session with a person who is struggling to forgive himself/herself, or maybe having a hard time forgiving another person. It is the poet talking to the client, but talking to all the rest of us as well. It is universal. It lets us know that someone else has been there too. And it is a good way to bring up a subject that the client may have been reluctant to talk about.

A male colleague uses my poem "No Geysers Lifted, Nor Flowers Bloomed" (p.28) with women who suffer from depression. This poem, written in a woman's voice, is immediately understood by them, and brings up issues involved in depression's genesis and treatment.

> I wanted to scream
> but the windows were open
> as my neighbor picked flowers...
>
> I wanted to scream
> but I had long ago forgotten
> how to bellow like a lion ...
>
> My scream became a yawn
> as I retreated to the safety
> of a goose-down comforter...

There are four stages in the process of using poetry for therapy. First, the client/reader must identify with the poem, feel that this poem has something to say to him/her. Second, the client examines the poem and discusses its meaning. Third, the client is asked to think about other meanings, and to compare and contrast these understandings. (Remember, this is not English 101. The bottom line here is not what the author intended, but what the client feels.) Fourth, the client is asked to integrate these thoughts into his/her own self-understanding.

There is a fifth unstated stage. It involves the therapeutic benefit of beauty, of art. When I read a poem of Mary Oliver to a client, or have it read to me, there is a moment when I let its beauty wash over me. It also happens when I lecture about poetry therapy and I read a poem aloud. Often I will read "To Roxanne" (from *In-Versing Your Life*), which is my poem about sibling rivalry, but also sisterly love. There is always a moment of silence at the end, when the poem is sinking in, when it transforms lecture into shared experience.

Children respond well to the poems of Shel Silverstein, Jack Prelutsky, and A.A. Milne. I have found that most traditional children's poetry is nature-based and does not talk about feelings, with the exception of the poets I mentioned above. I have found it more helpful to write my own poems which I use with children as young as three years old.

An example of a writing exercise that works well with children of all ages, is to assign a metaphor poem, such as "My Home" (from *In-Versing Your Life*). *I* ask them to write, "my home is like ... ," or "love is like ... ," or "I am like ... ," and then to make a list of metaphors which describe different aspects of the word assigned to them. This writing exercise is diagnostic as well as descriptive. I asked a ten year old boy, who would not talk about why he had been acting out, to write, "my home is like ..." He chose instead to slightly change the subject.

> His fist was like a hammer.
> His fist was like a missile.
> His fist was like a boulder rolling down a hill.
> His fist was like a subway train speeding along the track.
> His fist was like a hand in jello against my stomach
> His fist was like a flash burning through my heart.

It is not uncommon that clients will write about things they will not talk about. Writing creates a distance between subject and client that feels safe. If they choose to share their writing with you, handle it gently. Begin by asking him/her to tell you about it. Here is another metaphor poem, written by a nine year old girl who tries to write about love in a positive way, but each line turns sour before the end.

> Love is like a cold fall breeze in my face.
> Love is like a daisy in an onion patch
> so lonely and unloved.
> Love is like a snowflake on my nose
> so cold and lonesome.

Abuse issues are some of the most delicate issues to handle with children and teenagers. Research has shown that children who are physically and/or emotionally abused do not develop their expressive language skills at the same rate as other children, and so are at risk for hiding their feelings. These children especially need the spoken and written word to help develop those expressive language skills. In the poems I write for children I use animal characters with human feelings, such as Millie the Owl who is afraid of the dark. They are then encouraged to think about poor Millie, who is awake only at night, and never sees the light. I ask them: What does she do? Who can help her? Do you ever feel that way?

With adults who have been abused I read the poems of Sharon Olds, Alice Anderson, Roseann Lloyd and John Caddy. These are powerful poems, and can only be used when the client is ready to discard his/her defense mechanisms, and hear and talk about reality.

Often I will ask clients to write any kind of poem they want, just to be sure they will write something when their feelings start to overtake them. The following lines were written by a 16 year old girl who was acting out sexually.

> If I had only one wish you know what that would be?
> For me to fly into the sky for all eternity.

This poem was a cry for help, a veiled suicide wish. I found out later in therapy she had been sexually abused by her father, uncle and brother. No wonder she wanted to escape. She kept writing poems and discovering more and more about herself. She brought them into session and it was rich and powerful material to discuss. Much later in therapy she brought in this poem:

> I looked in the mirror and what did I see
> but the face of myself that was nothing like me.
> The face of a stranger covering my own
> had entered my body. Was I its new home?
> I studied this stranger for many days
>
> till at last I realized it was going to stay.
> I soon grew to know it and like it as well.
> What would others think? Only time would tell.
> I started to change in other ways too.
> People said I looked different. I said *I just grew.*
> I was now a new person. I took on new trends,
> and my stranger and I are now best of friends.

At the end of therapy with this young woman she had a notebook full of poems to mark the milestones of her journey toward health. This is another of the advantages of poetry therapy. We can carry a poem in our pocket, and take it out to give us motivation or courage, or to help us remember where we've been or where we want to go. People say that poets are "out in space", but in reality we are grounded to books and words and pieces of paper and pencils. And we love the sound of internal rhymes and heartbeat rhythms.

Alice Walker has a poem called "How Poems Are Made: A Discredited View," (*Her Blue Body Everything We Know.* 1991. Harcourt, Brace, Jovanovich: Orlando, FL p.335.) In the poem she says she understands how poems are made:

> There is a place the loss must go.
> There is a place the gain must go.
> The leftover love.

Poems, like dreams, deal with the leftover feelings. It's also what therapists do. Poetry helps me do my job. It helps me offer to clients, and to myself, a place for loss, a place for gain, for the leftover love.

I. LOOKING BACK

12

NAMES

The Asplundh tree man,
sinewy, with bark-tanned face,
calls me Ma'am

Doesn't know I am a Swede
same as Mr. Asplundh,
doesn't know my name

He asks me to sign
to clear cut my trees which
dare hang over Swepco wires

I won't sign,
make him show me the limbs
he is required to cut

I listen all day to buzzing
and watch the trees,
listen for the whine of the
wind

Then head my wheelbarrow
for piles of broad limbs
just right for my fireplace

He says, *This is junk,
can't burn pine,
don't waste your time*

I load a white log and say,
This is river birch,
he shrugs his shoulders

I pick up poplar, oak
more river birch
and a little pine won't hurt

He thinks they are the same,
trees, just trees,
to cut out of the way

Like cancer
or a poison ivy vine
that chokes out life

His nametag says Mr. Brown,
but he does not know me
and he does not know the trees

And he does not know
Mr. Asplundh
the Swede from Chicago
who called tree limbs "quist"

And he does not know
that in Mr. Asplundh's tongue
my name* means
"blooming limb"

*Blomquist

Who Are You? What Does Your Name Mean?

The poem "Names" reveals that my maiden name in Swedish means "blooming limb." I like that image of a green branch with flowers on it. My first name, Cynthia, means "reflector of light." I feel I am growing into that name.

What does your name mean, or who were you named after? Does your name fit you? Sometimes people take on new names when they feel that they have changed in some way. If you were to change your name, what would it be? How would that name reflect who you are?

Write a limerick using either your real name or your imaginary name, and tell who you are.

There once was a woman (or man) named ………....(rhyme A)

who .... (rhyme A)

and she/he ....(rhyme B)

and also ....(rhyme B)

that wonderful woman/man named ....(rhyme A)

I HEAR YOU LAUGHING
on the anniversary of my late grandmother's 100th birthday

This birth month, April, never brought you laughter.
Spring meant long days of hoeing and planting, sewing for Easter,

filling pots and bowls of food for teams of hired men, tired,
hungry from working and warming newly-thawed earth.

You could have celebrated with us today, cheered and sung,
but you chose to stop eating four years ago, said farewell

to your children, grand and great-grand, to doctors, to your garden
of strawberries and roses, and to your window wall of violets.

If you were here today I know you would shush the singing,
re-cork the bottle, accept only gifts of flowers and food

and we would remark how your longevity is due
to hard work, no pampering, and oatmeal each morning.

In today's thaw I cannot stay inside, my window of violets
pales at the sight of azalea hills in this Oklahoma town,

alongside redbud and dogwood, their blossoms light and lovely
as the baby blankets you quilted from left-over flannel.

Can you see these southern flowers through my eyes,
blooms that never flourished in Minnesota?

Cold nights denied these flowers in your garden,
just as your northern chill negated frivolous life.

I hear your voice, your laughter, (How could it be laughter,
you never laughed?) but I hear it plain,

and now again. I stare at crimson tulips, bulbs transported
on vessels from overseas, blooming in this foreign soil.

Just as your mother survived the tall ship journey,
your laughter navigates across the expanse of time,

and I understand how it is possible to transplant joy
to one another on this day in April, a day of budding.

Family of Origin

Who do you come from? Do you look like anyone in your family? What about your personality? Do you see characteristics passed down from generation to generation? My Grandmother was a stoic German farm woman who didn't laugh very often. But in my mind I heard her laugh four years after she died. I looked at the calendar and realized it would have been her 100th birthday that day. Are you "haunted" by your ancestors? Did any of them have physical disabilities? What did those relatives give you to make you stronger in this world? What did they pass on to you that makes it harder to live in this world?

Write about one person in your extended family who has influenced you for better or for worse. What did you learn from that person? What would you like to say to him/her? Write a conversation poem in couplets. First two lines could be you, and the second two lines are his/her reply, and so forth.

TOTEM POLE

Grandmother's golden brooch, the brass fish
Grandfather made, Step-Grandma's poetry
book,   Father's bear, Aunt's necklace

When I am
old and have
little room,
only these
possessions
will surround
me, spirits of
my genealogy.

Death allows
me to hold
them near,
wear their
souls around
my neck,
command their
living presence.

Grandfather's
fish, so heavy
it takes two
hands to hold,
spreads wide its
ashtray mouth,
but cannot swallow
burning ashes.

Father's bear,
roughly carved
with an artist's
steady hand,
chronicles
lost years with
layers of dust
in oak grooves.

Her life cut short,
too few times
Grandmother
wore this brooch
on foreign tours
of concert halls,

gold reflecting
glitter of music
stage and lights.

I don't remember
Step-Grandma's
voice, her silence
never a choice.

Her degree
held quietly,
she taught me
Poe and Yeats
from this leather-
bound book.

Her daughter
writes poems
which I have
never read.
Instead of verse
my aunt sends
a turquoise Indian
necklace.

For me she has
become the
silver spirit
of the necklace;

her mother, the
elusive muse of
the leather book.

Grandfather's fish
rests on my desk.
He cannot breathe.
He cannot forgive.

Grandmother's
brooch, pinned
to my breast,
insures music
will not end,
as Father lies
at last at peace
within the totem
of his wooden bear.

Support System

In the poem "Totem Pole" I wrote about all the people who, for various reasons, were not supportive of me. But I received support from the totems (the things they left behind) that represent those people. Who do you go to for support; family members or friends, institutional supports such as church, social workers, school etc? Do you have any objects that you cherish because they belonged to a loved one? Think about all the different kinds of support that we need: emotional support, companionship support, financial support, spiritual support, and for some of us, physical support. Do you feel that instead of getting support, you are giving support to too many people?

Draw a circle with YOU inside it. Write the names of people on the outside of the circle. Draw a line and arrow out to the names of people who you are supporting. Draw a line and arrow inward from the other person's name to you if you are receiving support from them. Are there more outward or inward arrows?

STEP AROUND

Life ain't been no crystal stair.
                    Langston Hughes

They try to make it into a stair,
crystal or no,
tell us we're moving up,
we're on the way, a step ahead,
up another rung,
until we reach a plateau
and where do we go
from there?

I say
we don't need to climb a ladder,
or get high enough to fall,
all we need to do is walk
together on this
flat-on-the-ground circle
stepping around
stones, entering
doorways.

                    ☐

Value System

Are your values the same as your parents'? If they are different, how does that affect your relationship with them? Do you feel guilty not climbing the ladder of success? Has your pain in any way shaped your value system? What is important to you that your family and/or friends do not understand? What is important to them that you find little importance in?

Think about what values you had as a child. Compare them to today's values. Do you feel as though you are on track, or do you think you need to return to some of your old values? Why?

CHILD/FAMILY VALUES   CURRENT VALUES

SOMETHING STOLEN

Prisoners used to wear stripes
(who cared if they defiled the zebra?)

but one too many must have run away
blending in with nature's cover.

Jails now send out work crews
in jumpsuits of neon orange

not matched in nature except in
Florida fruit and October maples.

That's why I bought the orange wool coat
that no one wanted, on sale for a year,

wool to warm the coming winter,
brightness to ward off approaching darkness,

reminding me of the orange heather suit
and angora sweater I wore the night we met,

bittersweet pinned in my cornsilk hair,
lipstick to match autumn's brilliance.

Now I wrap the warm coat around me
as I pick pyrocantha berries and hunt

orange mushrooms, remembering
not prisoners, but something stolen.

☐

Grief and Loss

In the poem "Something Stolen" the writer remembers an old love, and how it was stolen from her. What do you feel has been stolen from you; health, finances, happiness, relationships, security, independence, a carefree attitude, freedom, naivete? Do you ever feel as though you are a prisoner to your illness? How do you break out of your "jail"? This poem was written all around the color orange. What color represents your pain? Why? Has the color changed? Is it brighter or darker? Think about the losses in your life. Which ones have healed, and which ones are still open sores? Have you openly grieved for all those things you have lost, or have you been "strong," stuffing them all inside?

Write a poem listing each loss, and begin each line with the words:

A tear for . . .

A tear for . . .

A tear for . . .

NOW THAT HE'S GONE

they say i'm strong
don't want to be strong

like an iron bar
don't want to be tough

like a green limb
i'm not young any more

like the scent of a skunk
please don't stay away

i want to flow like liquid chocolate into the mold of your soul

and wrap us in
crimson cellophane

the hollow inside
large enough for two

☐

Lost Love

Are you still grieving a lost love? Did your physical pain have anything to do with losing this special person in your life? Is there some other reason the relationship didn't work? Does your pain affect your ability to begin a new relationship? Rejection, from someone you value highly, is one of the worst losses that a person can endure. How strong are you? Can you make it on your own? Do people tell you that you are strong? Do you believe them? What does "strong" mean to you? How long can you grieve over someone who is not coming back? How do you know when to move on?

Write a poem entitled *My Chocolate Heart*.

REINVENTING

These wheels cannot go where he needs to go, wheels narrow
as bicycle tires, but not free wheeling, not free, as his legs used to be.
These wheels hold a chair, pushed only on flat surfaces,
not weedy places of tall grass or ascending rugged rock.

These wheels cannot take him into Redbud Valley,
where gnarled roots and sharp boulders block access
to the new boardwalk path, designed by an Eagle Scout
who doesn't know anyone who cannot walk.

Other wheels drive him home, past planted azaleas,
dogwoods, neat beds of pansies, bright reds and yellows
of cultivated plants, dark green fertilized lawns,
the yawns of Sunday sitters, and chatter of house sparrows.

These wheels cannot go where he needs to go,
to gushing cave springs rushing down rock,
beyond city-paved trails where others politely smile,
move out of the way, and are secretly glad it isn't them.

But they don't know this: That even the feel
of smog-filled wind or the sound of a simple sparrow's song
jogs the joyful memory of the rush of wild running,
the whoosh of his blood, the hush of his hurried mind.

□

Special Loss

In the poem "Reinventing" I write about what happened to my husband after a major car accident which put him into a wheelchair for the rest of his life. One of the hardest losses for him was that he could no longer get into wilderness areas. It seems at first to be inconsequential in the face of all his other problems, but it was major. Is there something you have had to give up that is not outwardly noticeable to others, but for you, it was a great loss?

Write a poem entitled *But They Don't Know This*.

DANGLING

Some of us feel pain
as a fishhook pierces a worm,
slices and squishes through flesh,
then pokes out the other side.

Some of us feel exhausted
as she dangles there, no place to hide,
not wiggling much, not even
hoping for escape.

Some of us feel rejected
by the prideful fish, as they
turn away, allowing crappies
to prod, poke and nibble.

Some of us give up,
but others maxi-wiggle –
until one of us –
or more than one –

escapes the hook, floats free,
binds her wounds in algae,
bobs upward in the water
and climbs atop debris

to find the life authentic
(free from smelly hands,
fish teeth, hook barbs)
a life of grounded movement.

□

Feeling Betrayed

Have you felt betrayed "by the big fish?" Insurance companies, doctors, employers have all passed you by in favor of bigger fish. How about spouses? How has family treated you? The feeling of betrayal is one of the worst feelings in the world. Sometimes when we are sick and feeling helpless, we even feel rejected by God. Feeling rejected always feels as though we are dangling on a fish hook, with the spear in our side, waiting to die. Take the time to write about this ultimate sadness. This is the time to allow yourself to feel that pain.

Write about it in a poem entitled *Dangling On a Barbed Hook.*

NO GEYSERS LIFTED, NOR FLOWERS BLOOMED

I wanted to scream, but the windows were open as my
neighbor picked flowers, the delicate pastel kind
that she'd set on a yellow checkered tablecloth
while her children had milk and cookies.

I felt the yell rise to my lips
like a geyser pool filling
before its shooting-up,
rising, steaming water
spinning into my throat,
until my lips plugged its escape.

1 wanted to scream
but I had long ago forgotten
how to bellow like a lion
with a haunting belly growl,
its neck raised, arched,
its claws carving into dried clay.

My scream became a yawn
as I retreated to the safety
of a goose-down comforter
and a dark, no-dream sleep
where no geysers lifted
nor flowers bloomed.

☐

Depression

Do you feel as though you want to scream, but it would just take too much energy? Have you forgotten how to scream "with a haunting belly growl?" Do you go to sleep instead? Has your pain or fatigue made that slumber into "a dark, no dream sleep?" Examine your own level of depression and determine a plan of action. Do you need to see the doctor about it? Do you need more exercise? Do you need more social contact?

Start at the bottom of this page and write your depression a letter. Describe what you hate about it, and also what you love. By the time you reach the top of the page have a list of actions you will take to get the flowers blooming again in your life.

HOLY WAR

You do not have to forgive
spotted deer who nibble tender
leaves from your apple tree,
or corn-borers who devour
your sweet yellow ears,
or ants who march into your kitchen
as soldiers in a holy war.

You do not have to forgive
birds who nest in your chimney
or families of moles who
mound your manicured yard,
unless you value nature;
unless in hunger you have ever
picked and eaten a wild berry.

And you do not have to forgive
the drunkard who smashed
your favorite pottery turtle
against limestone boulders
in your rock garden, leaving
injured bloodroot and torn
hepatica to stand alone.

You do not have to forgive
that soul who left shattered
clay for you to find, broken
shards among the perennials,
unless you seek inner peace;
unless you have ever thrown
a valued vase against stone.

☐

Forgiveness

The poem says you do not have to forgive unless you value inner peace. That's a tough rule to follow. Who do you need to forgive? Is it your parents who didn't understand you, or the spouse who left you because he/she couldn't stand the complaining and fatigue any more? Is it the best friend who doesn't call any more, or the adult child who has forgotten you? Is it the doctor who discounted your pain, or the nurse who treated you as if you had a mental illness? How about your landlord who won't make any more exceptions for the late rent check? How does understanding lead to forgiveness? Can we forgive if we never understand? Are there times when you blame yourself having this pain, or for not treating your body right? How will you forgive yourself?

Write an answer to that question by writing an acrostic poem starting with the letters:

F

O

R

G

I

V

E

N

E

S

S

CHRISTMAS CHILD

I remember a Vietnam war vet who couldn't forget
what he learned. Saw too well where hell stood,
close enough to be smuggled in by dog, child or woman:
hell lurking at fence-end, between rows of a green field,
outside an open window, by the mailbox, in his guts.

I listened to him one Christmas morning muttering
how he threw away his Shetland-pony-and-picket-fence life,
his wife, kid and farm where he had it made, land paid for,
and even the friendship of old hometown folks
who never forgot his touchdown on Homecoming.

Now I am like him. Can't sit with my back to a window
or drive to the grocer's after dark. Can no longer control
my heart's pounding as I hear a car approach. I choose not
to plug in Christmas! red! blinking! lights!
and I distrust guardian angels who sing of peace.

I cannot forget. I still see the car rounding my street,
screeching its brakes, a thief demanding Christmas money,
the hands of a child jerking a silver gun, holding it to my face,
twitching, holding it like something hot –
blinding in intensity, brilliant as the Christmas star,

but much, much closer.

☐

Post Traumatic Stress Disorder (PTSD)

PTSD happens to victims who have experienced all kinds of trauma, not just veterans of foreign wars. How traumatic is this illness/pain for you? What were the events that led to the illness? How traumatic is your pain? How have you been treated by the medical profession? By your family? How intense is the pain? Are you having dreams about the trauma? Flashbacks? Are you afraid to go out? Do you feel as though you are a wounded veteran? Is there a holiday in which you associate the trauma, and therefore relive it every time the holiday rolls around?

Pretend you are a reporter for the PTSD NEWS. Tell us your story.

II. THE PRESENT

DOUBLE HELIX TWISTING

1. Monday, last year

I wanted to be the first just once
            to explain the alien,
            John Glenn in orbit
            describing spaceship earth,
Until now, when you phoned
            and told me about the lump,
            how it is present
            at your morning shower

And still there at your desk,
            how it walks with you
            down long hallways
            in your nods and hellos,

How it overtakes the blind night
            and becomes implanted
            in your inner vision
            as it sleeps with you.

The language of doctors
has become your new frontier.
            Each sunrise burns
            with radiation.

My hands cannot reach
            your new horizon.
            My calls cannot bridge
            the distance between sisters.

I lift my wristwatch
            upward in an arc
            through empty space
            to my eye's plain

And follow the predictable orbit
of its second hand
as I listen to the
Timex ticking.

☐

2. Monday, this year

Machine compressed
my breast between
glass plates, squeezed
flat for better imaging.

I dress. The tech
develops dark film.
I remember Mother,
how the nurse

did not let her leave,
with chill voice, "Go
Directly to Hospital.
Do Not Pass Go."

And my sister too,
how she was cut
on the surgery table
within hours.

The tech says, "Go."
Relief floods muscles
and breath. For today
I am well.

☐

3. *Saturday*

The envelope from St. Johns is routine I say,
but NO. I reread the halting words:

Breast imaging indicates need for
additional evaluation.
Does not mean serious problem. Should
not be ignored.

My Lord! I call the doctor.
Too late.
Saturday. Forced to wait.

☐

4. *Sunday*

My mind hurls through space
and cannot stop ticking.
I pray without ceasing
in my garden's cool light
pruning October's perennials for winter.

☐

5. *Monday, second week*

My phone connects first.
Nurse answers
at 8AM.

At 1 PM
I'm to come
tomorrow for ultrasound.

☐

6. *Tuesday*

I know this place, where to park,
where to sit.
The registration nurse recognizes me,
a returnee, like a teen
who fails her driver's test
seeking another chance at control.

The ultrasound clicks as the sensor
picks up what is wet and what is dense.
Gliding slick over my breast,
nothing hides
from vibrating waves of sound.

Two more days will pass until
the doctor knows
what has been found.
I feel my breath
sucked downward
into an unknown black hole.

☐

7. *Wednesday*

My thoughts turn to funerals.
Would the church be
full like Dad's,
or empty as Grandfather's?

Would they bury my cancer flesh,
or like the old tree

with Dutch Elm disease,
let the authorities dispose of me?

☐

8. *Thursday*

I listen to a radio show
of cancer survivors,
some lopsided, some
without hair, not
caring any more
about beauty,
I hear them talking
freely about living
without breasts,
living without fear,
living.

☐

9. *Midnight Dream*

A double helix twists and bends,
  dark green
      descending through space.
A whiff of Christmas pine
    from this garland's
        ticking dance of time
    sends my restless legs
        into a counterpoint
        of stretch
          and kick.

☐

10. *Friday*

I come home after six
to the phone message:

Doctor wants to see you.
Call for appointment.

Again too late. I scream
and scream and wait,

my stomach aching,
my head dizzy, not

prepared for this
galactic spin.

☐

11. *Saturday*

The insurance letter says:
This is to inform you
you must change
your primary physician.
Your present doctor
has been dropped
from our provider list.

I have been dropped
into a primordial goo
of dust and water.
I am an unstable isotope
seeking union,
seeking neutrality,
seeking.

☐

12. *Sunday*

I read "Atlantis."
    Mark Doty's poem
    goes beyond where
    I think it will stop.
This poem too,
    like the past
    summer's drought,
    extends itself into
    dry cracks of earth.

☐

13. *Monday, Third Week*

She enters with a clipboard,
her forehead drawn,
her eyes intense and
staring into the child in me
who feels a scolding coming on.

One, two, three,
Look at me.

Two are cysts, positioned at six
o'clock and four.

Loose, soft, no problem she says, as
her
fingers search through
a universe of flesh.

Number three
Look closer at me.

This one at three o'clock is
different, a trinity
of non-clarity: free-roaming,

soft-tissued,
but containing foreign matter.

Four, five, six,
See Dr.Hicks.

She calls herself conservative,
wants a second opinion,
a surgeon to feel, and maybe
cut, but I am
a liberal, open only to thought.

Seven, eight, nine,
You're probably fine.

I must decide about biopsy,
or about waiting three months,
about what resides in my body,
about cutting
away, or allowing to stay.

Ten, eleven, twelve,
Dig and delve?

☐

14. *This moment*

The double
helix twists
and bends
as biology
dictates.

My orbit is not
so predictable,
and I have discovered no
worm-hole
shortcuts.

I wait.

☐

Medical Treatment

In this poem, the narrator tells us that it took three weeks to find out a partial diagnosis for an illness that was terrifying to her. How have doctors and nurses treated you? Have they told you it was "all in your head"? Have they told you that you are just lazy? Have they treated you as a child, not giving you the information you need? Have they given you the run around, because no one wanted to treat your illness? Have you gone from specialist to specialist, each prescribing medicines that may or may not have a negative effect on the other meds you are taking? Have they taken their time to tell you the results of tests? When you go to the doctor's office, do you feel as though you are entering a war zone? Have you tried alternative medicine? What has worked? What has not worked?

Write a letter to the local American Medical Association (AMA) and chronicle your experience. Tell them how you felt during this vulnerable time in your life. Also tell them how you wish to be treated.

Dear Doctors:

WHAT MY FRIEND TOLD ME

I am eight years old and slipping on my boots
wondering whether the snow will melt
and lightning scorch the skies when
the world ends today.

Who set this date, sent out this warning
so all of us in the know are prepared,
like a girl scout working on a life badge
before the world will end?

And why are Dad and the neighbor
going to their jobs, the bus driver greeting
us with the same noble smile on this day
the world will end?

We all come to school unprepared
for our lessons. The teacher doesn't
understand. She says *We won't know
the time when the world will end.*

We wait. My feet fidget up and down.
My fingers turn cold. I do not hear
what the teacher is saying. I am afraid
what will happen when the world ends.

I ride home on the bus, its wheels gripping
and slipping on the slick pavement. I know
it's coming as I push away my dinner which
I won't need when the world ends.

Mother says *Don't go to bed hungry*, as she
kisses me and tucks me into the bed in which
I know I will spend my last moments
of terror when the world ends.

I fall asleep praying I will see Mother again,
and Teacher and Bus Driver, and snow and ice.
I awaken to the smell of eggs, broken and
frying in lard, yellow yolks hardening.

□

The End of My World

Do you feel that the world, as you used to know it, has ended? Is this really a new world, or just one in which the circumstances have changed? This poem about my fears as a child of the world ending is really a poem about hope. The world hasn't ended yet, even though it seemed likely many times. What are you discovering about this new world you live in? How are you fitting into it? The mother in the poem says, "Don't go to bed hungry." What have you learned about surviving in your world?

Write a poem with the following lines:

I never ...

I always ...

I try to ...

I am learning ...

I know that ...

I love to ...

I need to ...

BEFORE THE FALL

Leaves, not bright enough to notice, still hang onto
branches as days darken and northern winds tease.

Today this green remains supple, onion skin
still weeks away. Red trims only the edge.

I look closer. Outer tips have already blackened –
crisped like peppered catfish in a Cajun skillet.

As night lengthens, life shortens and
cell by cell, death begins at the edges.

☐

Inside Feelings

Do people look at you and wonder what the big deal is, why you are always complaining, and why you seldom get things done? Do you look good on the outside, but feel terrible inside? The leaves in this poem are just beginning to show the outward signs of fall. They must feel something inside, feel some kind of change or paralysis or pain, but we can't see it yet. Do you always find yourself having to defend your actions, or having to teach others what is really going on in your body? How often has someone called you "lazy," or "unorganized," or "not caring enough," when you thought they knew you and should understand?

Write a poem entitled *I used to be green and supple, but now... .*

LOOKING FOR NORMAL

I'm in a tizzy,
forever busy.
Deadlines are past
but I'm still on *fast,*
still in shock,
around the clock.
I take cold showers
every two hours.
I eat chocolate bars
and play my guitar.
I go out to lunch
with the "old bunch"
but I'm not hungry.
I'm much too angry.
So I play loud music,
please excuse it,
and read a book, but
my brain won't look.
I take a fast walk
but I need to talk.
No one understands.
I wring my hands.
I want to scream, "I'm
stuck in a bad dream."
It's all too formal.
I need normal.
Where'd it go?
I'm desperate to know.
It's time to move on.
Normal's gone.

☐

Fuzzy Brain

This poem was written about the way many of us feel when we are grieving a loss. With a chronic illness and pain the response to loss is more one of fatigue, not busy-ness. However, the other characteristics, anger, brain fuzziness, misunderstanding, might be similar. Do you take medications that make your brain feel as though it is moving in a fog? Even if you do not take medications, do you sometimes feel so over-whelmed that your brain can't take it all in? Stress is a big part of living with any illness, and being overly stressed can make us accident prone, forgetful, can cause word and thought blocking as well as general brain fatigue. How can you reduce the stress in your life?

Draw a bull's eye below and write the word "stress" at the center. Around the outside list some things that you can do to reduce stress in your life.

BOILING POINT

With each word

GOD

turns up the heat, but

DOESN'T

teach us how to

GIVE

and take, until the blood of

US

black and blue and red is

MORE

deadly

THAN WE

bubbling and bursting

CAN

in our hearts

ENDURE

☐

Anger

What are the things people say to you to supposedly make you feel better? How do you like it when someone says, "God doesn't give you more than you can endure?" It infuriates me. How about, "It'll make you a stronger person in the end"? or "God gave this to you for a reason"?

Do you ask yourself, "How much more can I endure?" When do you get to your boiling point? What do you do with your anger? Do you take it out on others? On yourself? Do you get depressed? Do you get sicker? What is a healthy way to let your anger bubble off? Do you ever try writing your anger down on a piece of paper and then burning it? Writing can be a wonderful way to get destructive anger out, and not hurt anyone in the process.

Write metaphors for anger, such as:
   my anger is a burning ball of oil rushing toward a dry forest
   my anger is like the wind of a tornado tossing everything, both good and bad, into a foreign land

My anger is like . . .

My anger is . . .

My anger is like . . .

My anger is . . .

COLOR COMMENTARY

1. Ball

From the stairway the room is dark:
formal tuxedos, lace and silk,
a celebration void of color.

This night swallows even
a diamond's sparkle,
tiny rays reflecting

red lips adorned within a universe
of black. One dance instructor
wears a purple gown.

☐

2. Funeral

Music drones from the organ,
sadder than the beige and gray clad
crowd, celebrating a life now past.

The old ones still wear black,
honoring another friend
whose light has dimmed.

The flowing vestments of the chapel
and choir are purple, long solemn
robes of deep, deep purple.

☐

3. Wedding

The door is edged in evergreen.
Her bridal gown of white is pure,
but trimmed of meaning.

Even guests now wear white
and mothers wear fashionable black
silk suits to make them look thin,

and bridesmaids never wear purple,
eggplant maybe, on a whim, dark
eggplant that appears black.

☐

4. Baptism

The water is clear, no color
yet reflected, until cheeks
redden, and lips turn purple

from the crying of one who seeks
only comfort and peace,
as the cold cross is fingered

on the baby's brow, and gently wiped
with Grandmother's
white, lace cloth, absorbing all.

☐

Does Life Seem Colorless or Black?

What used to add color to your life? What happened? Does each day seem colorless, each one like the last one? Why? Where is the color? Is there purple in your life? Where? The poem ends with the color white, all colors united. Where do you find color and light? Does life have to be colorless or black? Think about what color or colorlessness means to you. What is your favorite color? Do you see that color in your house, or in your clothes? What does that color represent? Have you changed your favorite color? Why?

Write a poem with a magic marker or crayon in your favorite color. Begin with these words:

I color my life . . .

BENEATH THE SICK-A-WAR TREE

Your sycamore branches, thick with hearted leaves,
don't cool a northerner in your smothering shade.

Beneath this canopy of southern hospitality
no grass grows, your heart allows only filtered light.

My child plays under your care, feels your burden
and names you *Sick-A-War*. We do not feel safe here.

I cannot explain my fast-paced voice, my choices,
my immigrant name, in this plantation world.

I am haunted by swaying limbs, and bodies who swung there,
whose color was wrong or whose lips would not keep silent.

I tread softly on your prickly soil, aware of land mines,
fallen seedballs, protecting your birthright with affliction.

☐

Safety

When I wrote the poem "Beneath the Sick-A-War Tree" I was a northerner living in Louisiana. I never felt as though I belonged there. My accent was wrong. I had no "kin" there. My politics didn't fit, and neither did my religion. Do you feel as though you are out-of-sync with your world, and you don't trust it to keep you safe? When have you felt safe? Do you feel as though you are under a "Sick-A-War" tree? What battles have you had to fight? Is there a truce in sight?

Write a poem entitled *Out From Under the Sick-a-War Tree.*

PATIENCE OF THE CROSS-TIMBERS *

Hundreds of years growing on a steep hill, desolate, aging
despite scarce nourishment, they wait for history to recognize them.

Crooked cedars, centuries old, twist in the shifting light of seasons,
and cling to a long forgotten hill shared by three-hundred-

year-old post oaks, every head cut off by lightning, every stump holding out
side limbs like wires on ragged and weathered clothes-line poles.

Recorded history reveals itself in the cross timbers' rings, some narrow
as a spider's thread, examined not by eye, but magnified to count

each period of drought, season of rain, each scarring fire, tornado, flood,
times of settlement and grazing. Washington Irving slept here

among the timbers, now a century older, and proclaimed them
beautiful. They have waited these years to hear it once again.

I wait. Transition is permanent. I understand these trees which grow
around rock and moss, trees which stretch limbs in crooked lines

seeking elusive light, trying to catch run-away water, clinging to life
long enough to leave a legacy on the land before becoming

firewood. Their endurance, spirituality of patience, their
mandala of encyclopedic rings. What they have is what I want.

□

*Remains of the south central old growth forest, called the Cross Timbers, made up
mostly of post oak and red cedar ranging in age from 300 to 1000 years old,
discovered in 1999 in Oklahoma.*

Patience

What have you learned about patience from living with pain? The cross timbers in the poem were very patient. It took one hundred years to re-discover their existence and their beauty. They don't look like other trees. They are gnarled and cut off. But their history makes them regal. What have patience and endurance taught you? What legacy have they given to you? Is there even one person in the world who sees your beauty, who recognizes your specialness? What does it feel like to be invisible in this world? How can you change that?

Write a poem entitled *The Spirituality of Endurance.*

THIEVES

Blasted pinfish
steals shrimpbait
meant for flounder
then pricks his pins
into my flesh as
I set him free –

It's Sunday on the dock
and I don't need his trouble.

I walk the beach
but receive no gift.
The empty shell
houses a hermit crab
who stole it first and
challenges me to a duel.

Thieves they are, refusing
to respect my ownership

of empty shell and shrimp,
of fish and ocean swell
and all the sands that
tumble and fall and shift
and scratch and finally catch
in my tight leather shoe.

□

Control

The poem "Thieves" is about control. We want it. We want to control everything in our life. But that never happens, especially when we live with chronic illness and pain. Quite often the tables are turned, and it is the illness that seems to be controlling us. What steps have you taken to be in control of your own health? What factors make that difficult? Is control important? What level of control? How does the concept of "letting go" fit into this discussion?

Write a letter to your pain. Get angry, tell it who's boss.

Blasted Pain ...

ESTATE SALE

Musty mink collars on coats of wool
emit bursts of musk when jostled.

Her silver, sparse and unmatched, her china,
chipped, show she had lived too long alone

in the white house across the street
where no one entered but the "go-for" man.

Last Christmas carolers sang outside
while she watched from her darkened den

and made no room at the inn for song,
nor light to brighten the dark night.

Now I watch the hunter/gatherers
shuffling treasures in and out

like tribes of hungry ants carrying
burdens too heavy for their frame.

They crawl over tatted lace,
framed photos of yellowed faces,

carnival glass, too gaudy
to use with formal china,

Reader's Digest classics, and
faded, embroidered sheets.

A sleek woman parks
a Jaguar adjacent to the sale.

She paws her way in,
surveys the territory,

then argues over a fur coat,
jumping at the jugular,

throwing coins, running
over ants, consuming the past.

Finances

Do you frequent garage sales? I once had a client who survived by buying things at one garage sale, and selling them for a profit at her own garage sale. Are your finances that tenuous? When a person is desperate they often resort to unsociable activities, such as grabbing for the last plate or dress or coat at a sale. Have you ever behaved that way? Why would a woman with a Jaguar car act this way at a garage sale? Have you ever given a garage sale, and felt embarrassed by the way people talked about your belongings? Have you learned how to bargain? Has your pride been hurt either as buyer or seller?

What is the financial burden of chronic illness and pain? Have you lost a job because of it? Have you lost medical insurance because of it? Are your drugs covered by insurance, or are they paid out of pocket? Has this illness pushed you toward dependency on the government, your parents or spouse?

Write a poem entitled *What I Will and Won't Do for Financial Security.*

RED FLAGS

It is summer's end as I survey the houses on my block,
and notice my home is not the only one sprouting
maple tree forests from its angular roof.

Each day generates inches in height, and roots
digging deep into the collected sludge
of my high-rise gutters.

The city plants trees in just-right holes,
trims and fertilizes them with care
and they turn brown,

but these air-born seedlings thrive, for now.
I know I must climb the ladder
and pull them out,

for they will die in winter's freeze,
and they must not become part
of a compost mix

that lures next year's seeds while they are young
and still flying high like Thurber's moth,
with sights on a star.

I'll wait to pull them out, until October,
so their leaves will redden
and line my silver gutters,

offering a salute to the neighborhood,
red flags flying high
waving goodbye.

☐

House and Yard-Keeping

Does your house or yard need work? Do you feel guilty because your lawn doesn't get mowed as often as the neighbor's? What about housework? Does pain or fatigue keep you from even the simplest tasks? Do you ever feel as though you will never catch up with all the work? What do you do about it? Do you have people who can help you do these tasks? How do you feel when you have to ask for help? Are you a perfectionist, or is it okay to "wait to pull them out, until October"?

Draw the four outer walls of a house. Now write a poem inside the walls about what it demands of you, and what you are able to give it.

MOVING ON

Our first home, cement, seemed a good way to begin,
set on the sands of Mokuleia, we heard waves smashing
into ancient reefs like thunder under a prairie sky.
Coconuts and clumps of dates dropped from tall clean palms.
When his army duty was done, we moved on.

In the North Carolina foothills we dropped our gear
into a Victorian home with a porch that wrapped its contents
like a long curling ribbon. It cost us next to nothing,
(locals wanted ramblers on mowed-acre lawns,)
but when we moved on, it sold for less than nothing.

Next we moved to a log cabin on Whitetop Mountain
where hikers on the Appalachian Trail were the only sign
of forward movement, and payment for services came
in creels of trout and jars of white lightnin', but we got sick
from the water, ran out of cash, and sold the cabin at auction.

Then to a stucco bungalow above a railroad changing yard,
where the upstairs wasn't heated and lilacs waited to bloom
until Memorial Day. Through the long winter we dug
a tunnel through the snow, not knowing if our car would start.
We moved across town to a real house on a lake

And a job which didn't work out and we sold that house too
and headed west to Billings, and a split-level beauty
with a yard full of flowers and raspberries, and a too-big sky
and too-independent residents unwilling to offer friendship.
We sold it two times, the buyers not keeping their payments.

Beneath live oaks and a fig tree we found our house in Louisiana
in an area called "transition," in a time of transition and we stayed
for five years until the kids learned the wrong things, and I stuck them
in the car, drove north, and bought a home on a Minnesota river
where I transplanted wildflowers and wrote poems under flying eagles.

Then we moved down river, to town, but it was also moving on,
becoming a suburb, each year losing more of its soul, and then
finally losing us to the city. I look for one more home, under an oak,
beside the berries, a house which can be bought, and lived in,
and maybe sold, a home with enough breadth to accept and then let go.

Transition

Do you feel as though you are always in transition? Always moving? Never quite getting where you want to be? Transition does not just mean moving from house to house or apartment to apartment, but also suggests a feeling of always being in the midst of change. Do you know what your goals are? Are they changing because of your pain? Has your profession or job changed due to this illness? Do you see things in a different light now that you have had to battle the medical establishment, family, landlords, bosses? Who are you right now? Do you like that person? Is it okay to be in transition? What are the constants (the things which do not change) in your life?

Take the word "transition." Write as many words with those ten letters as you can find. (Such as: ran, sit, on, stir, rant etc.) Then write a poem about your "transitions" and "constants" and try to use all of the words.

TRANSITION

III. LOOKING FORWARD

THE LONE WRITER

I came alone to the café.
In one corner were business suits,
gray, black, a little wine—
they dined with charts,
used only the right words
and ate proactively.

In front of the hearth
bridge clubbers
pointing with polished
nails, replayed their
morning's hand
between bites
of broccoli quiche.

I came alone to the cafe
and while I waited
the wizened crew,
not really wise, but tired,
and retired, refilled
their coffee cups and stories
with a new day's brew.

Black-clad artists,
around a window seat,
traded verbiage
about cloud shadows
sliding over the river,
darkening already
muted autumn hues.

I came alone to the café.
The waiter sat me
between the bustling
kitchen and coat closet.
I ordered garlic soup
and crumpled noisy
crackers over the
compatible characters
of my yellow writing pad.

□

Creating New Community

What do you do when you feel alone, as though you may have lost your former connections and community? Do you accept loneliness, or are you active in changing your situation? Here are some actions that might help; call a new or old acquaintance, attend a support group, develop a new hobby and find a group that shares your interest, go for a slow walk along the river, talking to those you pass along the way.

List the ingredients in a recipe for creating friendships:

A cup of . . .

A pinch of . . .

Whip together . . .

Heat slowly . . .

Blend in gently . . .

LIMERICK

There once was a girl from Stillwater
Whose father quite often caught her
Just going to bed
As he toasted his bread –
This night-owl doctor's daughter.

☐

Out of Sync

Is it hard to keep or establish friendships, or jobs, because your sleep schedule is out of sync with everyone else? Are you sleeping when they want to walk with you, or meet with you? When you force yourself to awaken for an interview or friend-date, do you feel jet-lag? The latest research about sleep is that 1) Routine is best, 2) Being awake during sunshine hours is not only best for treating depression, but is probably healthier for us all around, and 3) We can change our body clock through practice. If your world is getting smaller, you may want to take action on this matter.

Finish this rhyme:

- Tick tock,
- around the clock
-
- Not just talk.

- Tick tock
- It's a shock
-
- Walk the walk.

- Tick tock
- In a fog
-
- Walk the dog.

- Tick tock
- Start the day
-
- It's okay.

- Tick tock
- On my way
-
-

- Tick tock
-
-

LIGHT AND SHADOW

A stink of creosote spans the abandoned railroad
bridge, now a gathering place for walkers,

fisher people and breeze-wishers. An old cowboy
says, *I ain't been et yet,* and points

to fish swimming below, schools of shiners
chased by bass, bass chased by gar,

racing in spurts to survive another day
in shallow waters at the top of the river dam.

I see a child and her mother send out fish line.
There's a big one over there, Mama, and her mama looks,

but finds only a bright shadow, a fish of light,
alive only in the imagination of her child.

Mama grumbles, is certain this shadow creature
won't catch her hook, won't fill her hungry belly.

The child dances on the old bridge planks
to the moving rhythm of the fish. I see this light,

trickster of children and old cowboys, flapping
like a flag in the watery reflection of the sky.

☐

Hope

What do the doctors say about your pain? Will it go away? Do you have to learn to live with it? What is your hope? Are there times when you feel better? Do you think it will ever go away completely? As Emily Dickinson says, "Hope is a thing with feathers." In other words, hope can fly away, and just as easily, fly back again. In this poem hope is in the eye of a child who sees a "fish" which is really only a light shadow in the water. Her mother, living in the world of reality, knows it will not "fill her hungry belly." But the child's excitement is real, and hope is real for her. How does hope, or lack of hope, affect your life? How do you regain hope when it is gone?

Write a poem entitled *Hope is a Thing...* .

TOO MUCH TO COVER

Not enough seconds even when I count one thousand one, one thousand two,
even when I think of Vietnam prisoners tortured for a colossal minute
counting one thousand three, one thousand four,
one thousand five, one thousand six,
pulling fingernails out,
one thousand seven
still too few
seconds

Not enough
of anything, of chocolate,
of roses, of air-born shoes for jogging
on crooked roads that lead to sore feet, not
enough roads for all the people who want to parade
like the strutting woman whose dress was not big enough so she
slit the back open to accommodate her rear, and wore shorts underneath it all

☐

Time Management

Do you feel there is not time enough in a day for you to get the things done that you need to do? Does it seem as though there are enough hours, but because of the pain and fatigue it never turns out that way? Do you feel there is not enough of anything; money, time, love, respect, fun? And conversely, are there times when an hour seems endless, even torturous? What does pain do to time? Is time your friend or foe? What do you do to make it speed up at those times when it seems endless? How do you extend it when there is more to be done?

Write a letter to Father Time. Tell him what you think of his steady tick.

PARK AND SHOP
After my son said that park and shop backwards was 'pohs and krap.'

at the Park and Shop
you come to be seen. you come to pose in clothes
with the right labels and step inside to shelves of crap,
cigarettes, booze, stems of 75 cent satin roses with
cardboard heart and space to sign your name or
your X.
at the Park and Shop

iron bars protect windows with faded pictures
of half nude ladies and their johnny walker red
posing for cowboys in jeans tight enough to make
them sterile. here they sell rolls of lotto tickets,
used ones underfoot, all hope of winning gone.
life's a gamble

for at night patron's designer label jackets
hide bullets and guns, no turn of the bin
for winners and losers, just a turn of the barrel
determines who gets
trampled underfoot
at the Park and Shop.

□

Luck

Do you feel as though you lost your life savings in the lottery? Do you feel as though you are an outdated ticket on the floor, stepped on by other customers? What do you think about luck, about the spin of the barrel? If life's a gamble, then do you think if you wait long enough you might win? How much of a gambler are you? What is the alternative to being trampled underfoot? Is there any choice in "luck?" As a consumer, is there another store you can go to besides the "Park and Shop?"

Write a poem entitled *The Barrel Spins and I... .*

SECOND STORY

I've met all my neighbors but the man next door,
no moving day cookies, no advice on hardware stores,

just Friday lawn service, maid on Monday,
mail through the slot, and no delivered paper.

I watch his car leave the tombed garage early
and come home after all color of sun is gone,

darkened window glass hiding his face
like the skin of eggplant surrounding green flesh.

Facing my house, his second story window,
always dark and filled with shelves of cacti,

overlooks my old redbud tree, hole-filled,
barely hanging on for one last spring.

This morning as I lift my bedroom shade I see
its budlike flowers gliding along each branch

like water lilies outlining a beaver trail. I feel
my neighbor's eyes, know he sees this one last show,

this sunrise burst of life in pink and green —
his gaze, a farewell to the only neighbor he knows.

☐

Relationship to Nature

Do you have a window that looks out over something beautiful in nature? Or is there a park, path or wild area near you that you visit regularly? Sometimes nature is the only thing that can heal me. Sometimes I just need a look, and at other times it takes the fresh air and stimulation of wind or rain, or my body making its way through tall grass and wildflowers to make me feel whole again. The poem describes a man who is a hermit, but even he needs nature for comfort. How does your body feel when you are out in nature? How are your emotions?

Draw a simple map of your town or county. Mark the natural places you like to visit. Make a plan to get to one of them every couple of days. Bring something back home with you, such as some dried pods or wildflowers or a beautiful stone

Then write a poem entitled *This earth I belong to... .*

AT THE PLACE OF NO CONVERSATION

She visits weekly
but understands
he does not know her

Her smile remains constant
though there is no
greeting in return

Returning is harder
with each trip
to the nursing home

Home seems so far away
at this place
of no conversation

Conversation here
is a touch
of the hand

Hands stiff
and becoming boney
getting cold

Cold eyes
she meets wide-eyed
with hope

And with hope
she brings this time
a guest

Who would have guessed
what Mack, her dog,
could sense?

Scent alone
does not explain
Mack's nuzzling care

Careful now
he licks the coldness
of this hand

Handles taut skin
rubbing the old man
with warm fur

Furrows lift
from the man's eyes
his lips grope to form words

Wordless too long,
he touches Mack,
Come Back

□

Supportive Animals

Do you have a pet? Research has shown that pets can be a healing tool. The love they give is unconditional. They don't care who you are, and they do not judge you. That's what makes them different from human friends and family. But an animal in the home can also take a lot of work, so keep that in mind. A wonderful thing about pets is that we can touch them. Touch is a human need and many of us do not get our quota. A cat curling on your lap, or a dog lying at your feet can be a tremendous comfort.

Write about your experience with a pet. If you like, you may try writing a poem in the manner in which "At the Place of No Conversation" is written. It is written in three line stanzas. The last word of the third line is the first word in the next stanza (with a little variation.) It is fun to write using special rules. I consider the writing of a poem to be a kind of puzzle in which I set the rules and then try to fulfill them.

THE LEAP

A squirrel juts across my rooftop,
shifts its lift-off spot two, three, four times,
then sails to far limbs, its faith beyond mine.

Did he think the leap, fear fatigue of flight,
recall the emptiness of air, was he aware
of distance, and dared it anyway?

Did I see hesitation, one eternal
moment of choice between wanting,
judging and jumping?

What propels animals to proceed against fear,
to pump adrenaline into muscles which
leap across unmeasured margins?

□

Fear of the Unknown: How Do I Proceed

What has kept you from jumping, from moving ahead, from taking a risk? What are you afraid of? Does your pain keep you from acting? If you try to jump what might happen? What has happened in the past? If you don't move ahead, what might happen? What "unmeasured margin" do you need to leap across? Think about your plan of action? How will you control your pain?

Draw footsteps on this page. In each footstep write one thing you can do to move forward on your plan of action.

About the Author

Cynthia Gustavson was born in rural Minnesota to a jazz musician and a waitress in 1947. She is the author of five poetry collections, several poetry therapy workbooks, and has published in numerous journal articles. She was educated at Gustavus Adolphus College, Boston University, Louisiana State University, United Seminary of the Twin Cities, and Oklahoma State University, has taught at Northeastern State University in Tallequah, Oklahoma, and Louisiana State University in Shreveport, Louisiana, and has been an invited lecturer around the country.

In her twenty-two years as a social worker she has worked in drug prevention, practiced individual and group therapy, and worked extensively with caregivers of the chronically ill and developmentally disabled.

Winner of a New Millennium Writings Award in 2002 and finalist for the Rita Dove Poetry Award from the Salem College Center for Women Writers in 2004, Gustavson lives and works in Tulsa, Oklahoma with her husband of 36 years.

More information can be found at www.cynthiagustavson.com